ENERGY
WORKER

A CALL TO EMPOWERMENT

— • —

LLOYD MATTHEW THOMPSON

STARFIELD

Starfield Press
Oklahoma City, OK

ENERGYWORKER: A CALL TO EMPOWERMENT
by Lloyd Matthew Thompson
Copyright © 2015 Starfield Press - All Rights Reserved

First printing 2015
Second printing 2020

Paperback ISBN: 978-0692397763

Starfield Press
www.StarfieldPress.com
Oklahoma City, OK

Akasha Shore
www.AkashaShore.com

DISCLAIMER: The information in this book does not substitute for medical care. Do not discontinue use of medication, or disregard the advice of your medical professional. This information is a supplement to any current health care treatment, and is not intended to diagnose or cure. Always consult your doctor. The author and publisher of this book are not responsible for the actions of the reader.

Cover design by Lloyd Matthew Thompson

ENERGY WORKER

A CALL TO EMPOWERMENT

CONTENTS

CONTENTS

Dedicated to every inch and iota
of this beautiful, grand Universe.

That includes YOU.

FOREWORD

ARE YOU READY FOR higher levels of happiness, peace, fulfillment, and abundance in your life—even if it seems like there is always something blocking you, or holding you back, or not working?

Are you willing and ready to change the energy within yourself so you can create more of what you want in all areas of your existence?

Does it feel like you're really, truly ready for something new on your journey?

If you're feeling a "yes" to these inner longings—especially if you're hearing a loud, vibrant, *soul-thumping* "YES!"—then *Energyworker* will be an amazing tool for connecting you with how to create new, higher experiences of your own energy.

Living in an unconscious world creates false illusions around our power. We form unconscious perceptions that anything outside of ourselves — a job, others' opinions, our economic status, a key relationship, our possessions — has power over our life choices and abilities. We move through life believing we have to change those things *out there* in order to find the fulfillment we seek *in here.* And to be fair, that is certainly one way to approach the equation!

But as we continue on our spiritual paths, and awaken to more of our unlimited power and endless energy, we open up to the truth within the illusion. *We are the creators of energy.* We are either consciously or unconsciously creating everything around ourselves. It is up to each of us to claim this power within our beings, and to declare that we are amazing, unlimited vessels of Divine energy having this crazy, wild ride of a human experience.

One of the hardest periods in my life was right before I discovered the power of my own energy. Daunting questions loomed in every area of my life: What career path should I follow? Where should I move to? When is my life partner going to arrive? How can I make more money? What is my life purpose?

I was ready for all of these answers and to follow the best possible path — just point me in the right direction! I would have done anything to get what I wanted; I was desperate for clarity and movement and inner fulfillment. But my energy was not yet in alignment with my highest and best good. *This was my work to do.* The answers were not to be found in a new job title or a certain location on the map; rather, the answers were waiting within that vibrant essence of our Soul energy that is always teaching us more about our unlimited possibilities. The answers were being safely held within the energy of myself.

I was being guided to understand how powerful I was in ways I never even realized, especially with my driving intentions, unconscious belief systems, and inner programming. All of those aspects of my energy—and more—were ready and waiting for me to take the reins and lead them to higher places of expression with the conscious use of my energy.

And so I did the work.

With ongoing effort, honest self-examination, and a willingness to stretch myself, I stepped into a bigger version of my own energy that was always waiting for me. *I was the energy source.* I was the answer. I just had to say "yes!" and accept that the energy was within me the whole time. And so I did.

Chances are, you've arrived at this book because you're ready for new breakthroughs around your energy, your power, and your life. This is a wonderfully exciting place to be on one's journey! And my friend, Lloyd Matthew Thompson, is going to give you wise advice, great examples, and insightful explanations of how you are a natural Energyworker. Lloyd has written a resource that will guide, assist, and push you into more of your being than you ever thought possible—and you may even find yourself coming back to re-read certain chapters a few times, just to let it all sink in.

As you are reading this wisdom, trust that you are receiving it at the best possible time on your journey, and that you are ready to own more of your energy than ever before. Open up to more possibilities about yourself and what you can create, knowing on some level that anything is possible when everything is energy. Claim boldly that you are here to be the fullest, brightest, best version of yourself in all areas of life—and watch out world! This book is going to be creating some *amazing* Energyworkers.

And so it is.

Namaste,
Molly McCord

MOLLY McCORD, M.A., is a bestselling author, intuitive astrologer, and modern consciousness teacher.

She is the author of seven books, including her bestselling memoir, *The Art of Trapeze: One Woman's Journey of Soaring, Surrendering, and Awakening*.

She supports others in their spiritual awakening process on her website www.ConsciousCoolChic.com.

Download her free 44-page ebook, *Guided By Your Light: Ridiculously Loving and Celebrating Yourself* at www.ConsciousSoulGrowth.com.

INTRODUCTION

DID YOU KNOW THAT energy is one hundred percent of the world you live in? Not ninety-nine percent. Not even ninety-nine point nine-nine-nine percent. One hundred!

Everything you see, everything you touch, everything you smell, everything you hear, everything you taste, and everyone you meet is nothing but energy.

Energy can create.

Energy can destroy.

And energy is fluid — it can easily be worked with, so that we may flow through our lives with the same effortless grace it demonstrates for us.

Notice I said *with* there. When working with energy, it is not a *control* of the energy, but a working *with* the energy. A partnership.

That is your biggest key to true empowerment, and I've told it directly, first thing. If you put down this book and read no further, you will be just fine as that simple truth simmers in the back of your subconscious until it reaches a boiling point, and you won't be able to help but notice how energetic everything around you truly is.

Or you could just keep reading, and let me show you the world as I know it and see it—for that's all I can do.

The rest is up to you.

Lloyd Matthew Thompson
January 2015

If you want to find the secrets of the Universe,
think in terms of energy,
frequency
and vibration…

— Nikola Tesla

• 1 •
ENERGIZE!

IMAGINE A VAST, ENDLESS ocean. This ocean is swirling and raging in some areas, still and silent in others.

As you watch, a brilliant light begins to grow from the center of this ocean, brighter and brighter, warmer and warmer, until it is the magnitude of a sun—a star. The light suddenly rises from the ocean quicker than the blink of an eye. The light still seems to be emanating from beneath the surface of the ocean, yet is clearly radiating from *above* the ocean as well.

The surface of this radiant ocean—both the churning and the placid areas—now begin to release the tiniest fragments, each smaller than a single molecule. The heat of the light slowly and seemingly randomly evaporates these tiny pieces of the ocean, as if giving them wings. Each droplet taking flight is an exact replica — a mirror — of the ocean as a whole it was born from. If you were tiny enough yourself, and on that droplet, you would perhaps believe that droplet *was* the entire ocean — as big as things could ever get!

Countless billions of billions of these fragments drift from the whole in every direction. Some continue on and on, while others begin to cluster together, reattaching themselves to each other, forming their own worlds, their own environments.

Yet as you move even closer to one of these grouped clusters, you see that the same light from the center of the original ocean (or at least the first ocean that *you* saw — who knows if that one was merely a droplet as well!) is also glowing inside this new cluster-world. Curious, you slip deeper and find that things are in motion within this world as well — swirling and raging in some areas, still and silent in others.

And out of this motion you see rising billions of billions of forms. You see the water shaping and reshaping itself into such an array of dazzling *things* at a rate that leaves your mind feeling a bit woozy!

Now you look down at yourself, and realize you are glowing in the same lit ocean-water you have been observing merge, evaporate, and re-merge around you.

You are the same.

You are made of the same ocean as these worlds you see forming before you.

You *are* one of the worlds which formed from the ocean.

And this is not a fable. This is not some nice little fantasy trying to make you feel special — you *are* special!

The light here is a symbol of awareness, consciousness suddenly realizing... itself!

The ocean represents the pure energy our entire Universe and absolutely everything within it consists of. Molecules and atoms are not the basest base of this place. Energy is.

Energy within energy within energy.

Everyone and everything that ever existed came from this energy, yet never left this energy, and still has not left it. Energy may shift and change and move, but it can never be destroyed. In fact, everyone and everything that has *yet* to exist is also already within this energy — it simply hasn't churned into being yet, from our time-bound physical perspective.

Getting too deep?

That's all right — none of that is really necessary to know or understand anyway in order to live on Earth and work with energy in your daily life.

The essence of it is, everything is made of energy. Hard things, soft things, solid things, liquid things, gaseous things, and even invisible things are simply energy in various forms and vibrations. The vibration, or rate at which a thing is pulsing, determines its qualities, such as hard, soft, hot, or cold. Even its color is determined by the energy pulsing through it interacting with the light (also energy!) shining on it.

I think nearly everyone is familiar with at least one version of Star Trek, whether they've seen one of the television series or one of the movies, and the way the characters in that world travel between their starship and the planet they're orbiting. In that series, they use a device they call a "transporter," which essentially deconstructs their bodies and equipment into energy, then beams that energy signature down to the surface of the planet, where it then reconstructs their energy back into the solid objects and bodies they were to begin with. In fact, when the characters on that show are telling the ship they are ready to "beam up," they use the command "Energize!"

While quantum scientists in our world are currently still working on that level of such concepts, they have already succeeded in beaming data through thin air from one point to another separate point without the use of wires or radio waves. Yet what is air? Don't you think transporting things through thin air still suggests there is a medium the data is traveling through to get from point A to point B?

Think of the ocean this chapter began with, and think of the data the scientists beamed as a fish. By swimming through the water, that fish could easily get from point A to point B, though the medium of the water.

And our story ocean symbolizes energy.

Because everything everywhere is energy, everything everywhere is infinitely and irreversibly connected. The scientist's data was energy, traveled across energy instantaneously, and arrived as energy.

Our physical bodies are giant antennas for energy. Each of our senses are picking up the feedback of energy and translating it to our brain and nervous system as scents, sights, tastes, sounds, textures, and feelings. In fact, without energy receptors, we would never be able to operate within this physical plane! We would never be able to find where someone has moved something or built a wall. We would never be able to tell if we were scorching our fingertips off on a hot tray of cookies coming from the oven, or if our head was comfortable on our pillow as we drift to sleep at night.

Energy we can feel, yet cannot see, we call emotions. Memories can gather up and mold energy into emotions associated with things that have happened in the past just as well as imagination can gather and shape energy into things that we desire to happen. When one holds these patterns of energy long enough, they begin to break through, or manifest, in the physical world that can be seen and felt. This is how repeating cycles in our lives occur, as well as how attracting our desires works.

When one holds on to and sits in energy and emotions from the past, that attracts the energy to create circumstances fitting those emotions around us once again, whether desired or undesired! In the same way, imagining or visualizing what one believes they *would* like will set energies in motion to create corresponding situations and bring it into the physical plane.

I specify the physical plane above because the usual phrase of "bring it into reality" that someone may be tempted to use can too easily place limits and restrictions on a thing. The energetic levels are every bit as "real" as the physical, solid levels we operate in, and the standard understanding of the word "reality" does not usually include these.

Things like this are what many are finding now need to be redefined as our understanding of the universe around us expands, and I believe the overall worldview is shifting more and more into including the energetic or quantum levels of this universe as an accepted and provable reality.

An excellent example of the way our visualizing past, present, or future literally affects reality is the way experiments have been done on competitive athletes. With electrodes and monitors hooked up to every muscle in their body, as well as the activity in their brain, the athletes were instructed to mentally run through the routine of their athletic event while sitting completely still in a chair. The results were found that merely visualizing and imagining they were performing caused every muscle and brain activity to fire and activate at the precise time they were needed, believing the athlete was actually physically doing it—the body knew no difference, simply from the power of the mind and the energy called upon!

Unseen, or intangible energy also plays a vital part in the health of our physical bodies. If energy is not flowing well or not flowing at all through the physical body, sickness can begin to develop—sometimes quite seriously and lethally. The use of "energy healing" to help keep these channels clear is more popular than it has ever been. More on these topics will be covered a bit further on in this book.

There is nothing that can be done without energy. Each and every one of us must work with energy in a multitude of ways every minute of every day. Even our dreams as we sleep are our brain's interpretation of energy we are processing on one level or another, applying symbols and images as it attempts to make sense of it all, as the brain has quite a habit of doing.

The simple fact you exist in this form, in this moment, means you are already a natural-born energyworker.

• 2 •
AFFECTED BY ENERGY

As STATED IN THE previous chapter, energy is everything everywhere, and also affects everything everywhere. There are so many factors of energy bouncing around us at all times that it's really very easy to become overloaded by all the sensations your antenna of a body is picking up on. Those who have the higher sensitivity of what is often called an *empath* are even more easily overwhelmed.

It is very important to keep in mind how easily "external" energies can influence our own bodies and emotions. This is in no way a handy-dandy excuse to justify laziness, irresponsibility, or selfish behavior. It is instead a reminder to look outside ourselves at what may be happening around us whenever we may be feeling uncharacteristically stressed or angry, often for seemingly no reason at all.

One of the biggest and most overlooked influences that can affect us are astrological and planetary aspects, such as when Mercury is in retrograde, or when a certain planet is in an astrological sign opposite our own personal astrological sign. We won't have the space to discuss all the many infinite combinations of astrological aspects that may influence us here, and there are many astrologists easily found who know much more about these than I do.

There are many, many people who refuse to give astrology any credit whatsoever, and dismiss it as pure hogwash, yet these same people readily agree that the ocean tides of our planet are pushed and pulled by the gravity of our moon as it orbits the earth. Doesn't it make sense that the gravity and energy of other heavenly bodies affect our planet and our own bodies in the same way? After all, our human bodies are between 50% to 75% water—we are little walking oceans ourselves! (Does this remind you of chapter one, perhaps?)

If the gravity of the moon orbiting earth can affect our vast oceans, which are water, why would it not affect our watery human bodies and emotions as well?

In fact, most everyone already agrees that the moon *does* affect our emotions. "Must be a full moon tonight," you'll hear people say. "All the wackos are out!" This is the pull of the moon taxing our emotional bodies — just one example of the way many planets and other phenomena among the stars can affect us. The word *lunacy* is derived from this association with the moon.

I used to be the manager of a 7-Eleven convenience store, and decided at one point to take advantage of the interacting with hundreds of people each shift it required, to observe the effects of the moon for myself. I kept close track of what phase the moon was in, and then watched how people were acting in relation. I had many regular customers I would see every day, so I even had a gauge as to what their "normal" personalities were like. What I observed was that every time it was a full moon — the greatest pull — people did in fact "go crazy" or act in more uncharacteristic and irrational ways. I also noticed there was more violence and crime in general citywide around the full moon.

Several years later, when I met my wife, who had worked fifteen years in the mental health field, she confirmed that it is a known fact among the mental health fields that most suicides, mental breaks, and violent crimes occur around the full moon. The emotional shores within our bodies are swelled like the tide, and some people are unfortunately tipped over the edge, where they cross their breaking point and snap.

I want to reiterate here again that these influences are never meant to be abused as excuses for bad behavior. Authenticity, and owning one's own actions are vitally important responsibilities for anyone wishing to grow and evolve and make a difference in this world.

Emotions, which are like gravitational pulls affecting all that is around them themselves, have long been associated with the element of water. Each card in the tarot deck's suit of Cups, which has been documented as early as the year 1430, represents all the many facets of our emotional natures. People also speak of "pouring their heart out," which suggests emotions and feelings are of a liquid nature.

When we walk into a room where other people are, we automatically sense the mood — or emotion — of the environment. If there is tension present, we know it, and if there is a comfortable lightness, we easily feel that as well.

In the same way, when we come into contact with another person one on one, we can instantly tell what sort of mood they are in without ever hearing a word from their mouth or observing any of their body language. Their emotional energy is felt by our emotional energy, and we recognize what they are radiating from our own personal experience with such emotions.

To blame the energy of others for our own actions and responses — even if we are legitimately picking up on and feeling the energy they are blasting out—is essentially the same as sitting down in a mud puddle and crying because our clothes are dirty, when we can easily just get up and clean them or change to a fresh outfit. The power, choice, and responsibility is always ours. "Every single person has a reason to sit in the corner and suck their thumb," is an expression in our household, and what we teach our children, meaning we can sit still and whine about something, or we can get up and do something about it.

The same applies with energy.

If we are feeling bombarded by the energy and attitude someone is crushing us with, the choice is fully ours whether to accept it and let it absorb into our own energy field so that we begin perpetuating the energy forward ourselves, or to put our foot down and decide, "Nope! Not today! Today, I am choosing to be *this* way instead." That alone will set the intention for your own energy to override and outshine the other energy, even if it only shifts for your own self.

In the same way, each of us are responsible for the energy *we* broadcast out. It is extremely important to mindfully choose what sort of energy and emotions we wish to radiate to others and the world as we go about our day. If we emit negative or angry frequencies, and those frequencies affect someone in our environment, tipping them over the edge of doing something *they* will regret or harm another with, where does that fault lie? Children and pets especially are little super sponges that absorb the energies of their environments so easily, and begin to reflect it back, whether in actions or physical symptoms such as sickness. There is no way to know how each of us affect another in either positive or negative ways, so clearly the best or highest action to take is to strive to be consciously aware of our own thoughts and actions at all times. Everything always begins with ourselves.

This is a never-ending task that is definitely hard work, especially as we expose and chip away at habits that have taken root over a lifetime of repetition. It would be a fantastic thing if "H.A." meetings existed—Habituals Anonymous—to help with these energy and attitude addictions, as we have meetings of that sort for other substance addictions. In fact, "HA" would be the perfect name for it, as one of the greatest and quickest energy shifters is laughter! Humor is a very important grounding tool.

But no one can ever change another person. That is something that only they can choose to do for themselves. Our own self is the only thing we have any control of, and when we are able to shift and maintain ourselves, we are able to withstand even the most negative energy barrages.

Whatever energy a person is currently sitting

in, they will not be able to see past it or through it until they are ready and willing to. Until they decide to change or are open to considering another view, they are right in their own eyes, and hold the absolute truth as far as they are concerned. No one can force them otherwise.

I was raised in a very strict Baptist household, where everything was firmly "by the book." I remember one time, back when the internet was first beginning to emerge, and chatrooms and message boards were the "in" thing, I had somehow met a person who proclaimed themselves to be a pagan. I was just as dead-sure I had the right view of things as they were sure of their own views, but I had ignorantly decided I was going to set them straight and fix them right up! Over the course of months, long emails were exchanged, each of us stubbornly arguing our points, and getting nowhere. Both of us were sure our points made inarguable sense, and neither of us were open to considering another view at that time.

I can think back to that now, in the light of where and who I am today, and see that that was a complete waste of time and energy — and even realize that I have come to agree with many of the things I argued against, through my own personal experience over the last twenty years. But until I was ready to open and explore more of the world around me, I could see nothing else, just as they could not, on their side.

Samsara is the Buddhist word for what we are all trying to break free of and attain enlightenment from in this life. Many misunderstand samsara to mean this physical world, as if the physical world is "bad" in and of itself, and we must get out of it in order to be free. This couldn't be further from the truth!

This physical world, with all its whirling and swirling energies is honored and seen as the most beautiful tool to free ourselves—a daily gym to practice and train in for the mastery of our own energies. It is considered extremely good fortune to be born into this physical world.

Samsara is not the physical world itself, but it is our habitual patterns and knee-jerk responses. It is the attachments, desires, and death-grips on control that we cling to—what causes our suffering and stumbling. Enlightenment and freedom *can* exist in this place, even in the midst of other uncomfortable energies.

When we commit to doing our own work—whatever work may be required in our own unique life scenario—to break our habits and empower ourselves by *joining* the world rather than trying to fight it as something outside of ourselves, we will find that we are free, and have indeed been free all along.

• 3 •
READING ENERGY

WORKING WITH ENERGY IS not something
magical anyone has to learn. It is naturally
ingrained in everyone already. If everything and
everyone is nothing but energy, the fact we can
detect where an object is located shows we can
"read" energy. The fact we can then actually pick
up the object and move it to another location
shows we can work with energy.

Reading energy is nothing more than sensing
energy. All our senses are made to detect energy,
whether we are reading energy with our tongue,
nose, eyes, ears, fingertips, or our intuitive
abilities. Our intuitive sensors include the ability
to "feel" the mood of a room or pick up on
another's attitude, as mentioned before. It is an
unexplainable knowing, yet every single person
alive can confirm they have personally done this

many times without ever thinking about it, or being taught how to do it.

But did you know one doesn't have to even be in the physical presence of a thing in order to sense it—or even in the same time?

For example, you may be sensing, or reading *me* right now, but am I directly in front of you at this moment? My body may not be present with you, but my *energy* is—in the form of this book! As you are reading these words I've written, you are getting a sense of what I'm like, where I'm coming from, and even the intention or heart behind the book. As I set these words onto the page, the energy of my intentions are naturally embedded within them, free for anyone to sense.

Have you ever wondered why you instantly "click" with some authors, and not so much with others? A book you don't really resonate with may be extremely well written, and have highly recommended reviews, but if your energy is not in sync with or matching to the energy of the author, you may find yourself having a tedious time trying to get through it.

This applies to anything anywhere—reading books is merely one example. Think of music that is masterfully performed or sung, yet you just don't "dig" it.

As I am writing this, it is currently early in the year 2015. You may now be reading this in the year 2043, and yet here I am with you in *your* time. We are not guaranteed to survive past this very hour, so my body may actually be dead in your time, and yet nevertheless — here I am with you now!

Additionally, I am writing this from the state of Oklahoma, in the United States of America, but you may be in Wales or Costa Rica, so we can also see that an author is not required to have been sitting in the very spot *you* are now sitting at in order for their energy to linger and be sensed by you.

These are examples of how energy is not bound by space or time.

When you receive an email or a text message on your phone, you get an immediate sense of its tone the sender has embedded it with. Mere letters on a screen cannot convey emotion or attitude in and of themselves, but the energy their creator cannot help but layer into them certainly can — and energy cannot lie. Even if someone is trying to write a letter that appears to be cheerful and fine on the surface, if the true root of the letter holds resentment, sarcasm, or hate, for example, the underlying intention cannot be pretended away and magically hidden. It is the same when interacting with others in person — one knows when another is not *really* "fine," even if that is what the other insists, when it is going against their truth.

When we do pick up on the energy and

emotions of others, it is incredibly easy for us to take on those emotions in our own energy field, and begin fostering and spreading more of the same to even more people's energy fields. This is one of the most important times when we must be as empowered and steady in our own selves as possible, fully centered and present, so that we are hopefully able to catch the moment this absorbing of energy begins to happen, and put a stop to furthering any potential harm.

It is vitally important to know yourself and to consciously recognize the feel of your own energy. The better you know your own energy, the quicker your internal alarms will begin to sound when an energy that is not your own begins to soak in. Once again, we see that everything begins with you.

When we know who we are, know what our own boundaries and limits are, and know that we are truly all right with who we are, then we are genuinely empowered, and find we have the strength to embody our own space, no matter what else is going on around us. This is what the Biblical quote "In the world, but not of the world" refers to—when we are self-empowered in this way, we are no longer swayed by the winds everything around us is blasting our direction. We do not become what we are bombarded with, even though we are in the midst of it.

Yet even then, as long as we are human, there will always be moments when we find ourselves overwhelmed by energies, or even lost in the flood of energy a trigger sparks within us.

The 2014 Walt Disney motion picture, *Maleficent*, portrayed this very well. The story in this movie was "the other side" of the Sleeping Beauty fairy tale, where we were shown the real reason Maleficent cursed Princess Aurora to prick her finger on the needle of a spinning wheel on her sixteenth birthday and sleep forever. Maleficent began filled with kindness and in tune with the earth and all of nature around her. Then the king, in his anger and jealousy, committed a wrong against Maleficent for his own selfish reasons. Maleficent absorbed those energies, which combined with her own pain and anger, and she became lost inside her own swirling darkness, eventually cursing the king's daughter in an act of revenge.

Without giving away too much of the storyline, I do want to assure you that wonderful movie also demonstrates that no matter what one has done, there is always a chance for redemption—each moment begins a brand new day and a fresh, clean slate. It's never too late, and love is the most powerful energy in the Universe.

My family and I experienced our own struggle to stay afloat in a sea of extremely infuriating energies over the past couple years. I, who have always considered myself very peaceable and caring, can personally confirm how easily other typically uncharacteristic energies can overwhelm. Even now, I am still working on and examining the hatred I feel toward those who endangered my family. Even when we work hard to shape ourselves how our Heart leads us to be, the heat of the moment can override all of it in the blink of an eye if we are not as solid in our empowerment as we can be.

I don't have all the answers, or even most of the answers with this. The only thing that can really be done is to keep moving on, with our visions and goals firmly in sight.

When we come to realize that an emotion or energy that we are feeling is not originating from us or is not one we wish to cultivate, we can only acknowledge what we are feeling, look to find the root or source of it if possible, and make the decision to alter it or remove it, and then continue on without beating ourselves up.

That is the beginning of working with energy.

WORKING WITH ENERGY

IF THE BEGINNING OF working with energy is learning to truly sense and identify what we are feeling within ourselves, and then taking up our empowerment and making whatever decisions are needed to change or enhance that energy as needed or desired, then the next step is naturally to practice sensing and interacting with the energies of the world around us in the same way.

What if, when you enter a room and sense that it does not feel good, instead of turning and running from it, you begin to fill the room with a more positive and healthy energy?

What if, rather than crossing your fingers and hoping that a certain thing will happen in your favor, you instead sent energy ahead of yourself, requesting that what you want be done in order to help you out?

What if, instead of watching and waiting to find something out, you were able to get a "sneak peek" sense of how it might be?

These are only a few things able to be done in working with energy—not to *control* the energy, but to work *with* the energy and go *with* its flow, tapping into its streams and essentially communicating with it. It can be as if you and the energy of everything are on a team together, complete with give-and-take conversation.

The same way you get the best results by cultivating a relationship with and by respecting another individual in order to work *with* them to come to an agreement on something, the same way you must develop a relationship with the energy of all that is around you in order to accomplish work with it. Some humans may be able to be bullied into submission to do another's will, but the energy of the Universe—which is *all* things—does *not* respond to that. Honor, respect, and authenticity are the keys to a personal relationship with the Universe, as well as gratefulness and humbleness. Trying to issue commands and demands in the energy of entitledness or a power-trip opens the door for suffering rather than assistance.

The language of energy is feelings and emotions, and the muscles of moving and shifting energy are visualization and imagination. You "hear" what the energy is saying by feeling the tone or emotion of it, just as you do when relating with another person, and you "speak" to it in return in the same way, communicating what you wish in the language of feelings and mental images. When you are familiar enough with yourself and your own energy, you will be able to tell the difference if the feelings are coming from yourself, or if you are sensing from "outside" yourself, even though there is not really any separate "you" and "them" when it comes to the energetic realms. Though everything and everyone is made of the same energy, each individual thing and person has its own energy signature, and it is possible to sense even the tiniest difference in signature.

If the energy of a room or building you enter is not-so-harmonious, you can take up your empowerment and quickly shoot out an emotional signal to the surrounding energy, visualize a portal opening overhead, for example, and invite a more positive, light-hearted energy to begin flowing into the room via that portal. This may or may not shift and tip the scales of the energy immediately, or even while you are there to feel it, but—as everything begins with yourself first—you yourself will be immediately shifted and able to handle the discordant energies, knowing that you've done something to begin a change.

If you are driving up an on-ramp to enter a

highway, and need other vehicles to scoot over or slow down to let you on, you can either try your luck and muscle your way in between them, or you can empower yourself and visualize and ask that a space be created for you to slip easily in line as you begin to enter the on-ramp in the first place—or better yet, visualize and broadcast your requests for your route before you even leave your house!

Try communicating with the energies ahead of you in the same way for finding up-close parking spaces in a busy parking lot. Perhaps the energy can be arranged for someone to suddenly get the idea to leave at the perfect timing of your arrival to claim their spot.

These are but a few examples of the limitless ways energy can be worked with in our everyday lives. After a while, these things will come as naturally to you as breathing, and you will barely have to think about beaming requests or adjusting an environment as you go along. The more you understand through personal experience all the ways energy works in our universe, the more you will realize just how interactive this world is—and just how empowered *you* truly are. No one is ever completely helpless.

It is also important to understand that if the things we request and visualize do not happen, it in no way means that we did something wrong or are no longer empowered. Never be discouraged if you do not see immediate results or get what you requested. There are a million different factors that could be the reason for something not happening — and no way to nail down exactly which factor it was that caused it to not happen. We simply shrug our shoulders, say, "Oh well — *that* one didn't happen," forget about it, and move on. We never give up.

In the same way that it takes effort, mindfulness, and practice to change a habit within ourselves, and change does not happen overnight, the things we request — whether our request is an adding or subtracting from our lives — may not happen instantly. There is often no "magical poof" in life. Most things take a bit of time as the energy arranges and rearranges — an ever-flowing river.

One of the most popular but most misunderstood teachings has been what they call the Law of Attraction. The Law of Attraction method is built on these concepts of working with energy, but unfortunately grows contorted or twisted as people try to manipulate it and use it as a magic wand to get whatever it is they desire. In its mainstream understanding, it has taken on quite a materialistic tone. It dances on the borders of trying to control the energies as if they were your minions or servants.

Working with energy is not about seeing what

you can get for yourself out of it. You may indeed sometimes get things or get your way by working with it, true, but the interaction must be a give-and-take relationship. We are only one part of the whole, not the master of the whole. What friend of yours would stick around if all you did was take, take, take? What sort of friendship would that be?

The true meaning of and keys to working *with* the Law of Attraction is to be in tune with *yourself*, and becoming a friend to the Universe. The more you are in tune with and know yourself, the more in tune with the energies and world around you you will be able to be, and then you will be able to "sync up" with your environment and flow with a natural grace, attracting all you need. Our needs are always met, if we allow them to flow to us unhindered and uncontrolled.

As far as our desires — things we want, but don't necessarily need — I've observed that it often depends on what is best for all involved whether we get that desire or not — and *that* is often determined from a "bigger picture" we usually cannot see until later on.

There is an ancient tale of a farmer whose horse ran away. His friends and neighbors patted his back and said, "What terrible luck! We're so sorry to hear this." The farmer replied, "Is it bad luck? Let's just wait and see — it's too early to tell."

A few days later, the horse returned with another horse at its side. The farmer's friends and neighbors rejoiced, saying, "Oh! You were right! It *was* good luck after all! Congratulations!" The farmer shrugged and said, "Is it good luck? Let's just wait and see—it's too early to tell."

A while later, the farmer's son was riding one of the horses, and fell and broke his leg. "What terrible luck! You were right again!" And you can guess what the farmer replied once more. "Is it terrible? Let's wait and see."

A few weeks later, the country went to war, and all the young men were drafted to join the army. The farmer's son was of course excused due to his broken leg.

In this story, the farmer naturally would have *desired* that his horse had stayed, or that his son hadn't been harmed, but later on, the bigger picture was always revealed to have been for the best all along, even if it didn't appear to be so at the time.

Another recent movie with such a well-done message along these lines is *Into the Woods*, the 2014 Walt Disney film adaptation of the Broadway stage musical. In this story, each of the classic fairy tale characters are seeking and scheming for what they think they want, as if the grass is greener on the other side of the fence. But the question is posed, "Is what you want what you really need?" The more we are in tune with ourselves and truly know the difference between what we want and what we need, the clearer our working with energy to manifest these things will be, and we will be much more careful and specific with what we ask for.

When we are putting requests out to the Universe or working with energy throughout our everyday lives, it is also very important to make sure we are not doing it from a place of fear. The energy of fear will shut off your relationship with the energies quicker than you can blink an eye.

Motives and intentions are extremely important in working with energy, and just as energy cannot lie, it also cannot be lied *to*. There is a definite difference between trying to arrange something in fear that your desire or something else will or will not come to be, and trying to arrange something for other more honorable reasons. You can't trick the Universe any more than you can mask arrogance and bullying as strength and wisdom.

The more you work with energy, the more you will automatically come to see that everything really does always work out for the best, in every situation. Everything is always all right. Things may not seem all right in the moment, if the reality does not match our expectations or desires, but when we reach the point where we are able to let it go and let it flow, we can more easily just wait and see what happens next.

If we are feeling the need or urging from our Heart for change, but have no way to make the change at the moment, we can begin communicating our desire to the energies in small ways, such as rearranging some of the furniture in our home, or changing the route we drive to work. This invites a shifting into our energy field, and begins to crack open any resistance to change we may be habitually holding. Even tiny changes can begin paving the way for bigger changes to flow in. Changing up our routines can help us begin to *feel* the energy of change within ourselves and our environment, and that can then be directed toward our request for the greater change we need. That greater change can then have a wider channel to arrange and flow into place, if that is what is truly best.

As mentioned before, none of these methods of working with energy are to be used to try to control *anything* — neither the environment or other people. Even when the shamans of old communicated with the energies of the planet to ask that rains be brought to the village for the benefit of the people, sometimes the answer was no. To attempt to use energy to control is a misuse and abuse of empowerment, and is operating from a place of fear. Love works with and respects all that is around, while fear tries to manipulate and control, in order to wrestle and manhandle desires into existence — and who can say what the true impact of bullying will end up being?

The energy we put out is the energy that will attract back to us. If we interact with our world in the energy of love and respect, allowing for the freedom of what will happen to happen regardless of our personal desires, we will find the same is returned to us, and a certain ease and flow will be seen in our lives. On the other hand, if we interact with the energy of force and control, what might we in turn be forced into? Our desires may have quite a difficult time flowing into a channel pinched off with fear and attachment.

• 5 •
INTUITIVE LIVING

As WE GO ABOUT our day, interacting with the different energies, we do not have to remain at the level of visualizing the energies as faceless, shapeless energy blobs or the like. The energy that makes up everything is just as alive and conscious as you are—you are the same energy, after all!

When you are communicating with and nurturing a relationship with the world around you, it is literally as if you are getting to know another person. There is energy exchanged back and forth, and a recognition grows as the two of you become closer friends.

Have you ever talked to your bed? Have you ever expressed your gratefulness to your house for sheltering you from the rain?

If these examples sound ridiculous to you, try

replacing the items in the above sentences with something else, and get a feel for the perspective of it. Does it seem so silly if you use the word *pet* instead? Talking to pets isn't considered so odd, so what is the difference whether you're talking to your cat or your bed? Aren't they made of the same energy?

It is the energy that is alive, and not the object the energy is making up that determines if it is alive—so what if your bed doesn't breathe or eat or move the way your cat does? Who is to say it is not just as alive as your cat? Perhaps it would like to be thanked for holding you up and protecting you as you sleep through the night, or even for staying in one place for you to be able to locate when you need to lie down. You may find it to be even more comfortable for you if you express your gratefulness to it, and in exchange, you just may get the best and most rejuvenating sleep you've ever had!

I personally have done this with my vehicles for quite a number of years now. I've found that respecting and being kind to the vehicle helps it run smoother and longer with fewer problems. Connecting with the vehicle as I drive it down the highway, I can feel or pick up on even the most subtle changes in its normal operation more quickly, from the exchange of energy between us, as if it were a conversation. It is almost as if the vehicle becomes an extension of my own body, reminiscent of the way the Na'vi on planet Pandora connect with the horses and dragons they ride in the 2009 James Cameron blockbuster movie, *Avatar*.

One time, I felt a slight vibration, barely noticeable, but felt or "saw" in my mind a directing toward the tires. Visually inspecting the tires revealed nothing amiss, but I took it in to the tire shop anyway, trusting what I felt. Sure enough, they discovered one of the tires had been about to blow out, and if I had driven around much further, it would have! Had I been unmindful of the energetic feedback and physical signs the vehicle was communicating, or ignored the intuitive nudge to have it checked anyway, the tire could have blown at a very dangerous time, possibly with the lives of my entire family at stake.

The vehicle doesn't offer only warnings or "negative" feedback—it also responds with "happy" feedback, such as when it's just had a good vacuuming or washing. Taking care of it even in cosmetic surface-level ways like this shows love and respect to it, and just like any living thing, it loves that respect, and gives love and service in return. Give-and-take!

This, of course, applies to everything everywhere. The car is only an example to spark the imagination and open the mind.

Before even buying a new vehicle, I connect

with the one I'm considering, and talk to it, feeling if it would be compatible and willing to serve and be a part of the family.

Respecting houses and buildings is an important thing often overlooked by many as well. Acknowledging the building or home, and asking permission to enter will establish a positive connection with the energy of the place from the beginning.

This is especially important if you are moving your residence. When my family and I moved to a new house, I made sure to keep both houses included in the process, talking to each of them, asking permission to leave the one, and asking permission to join the other, and asking that the energies of each help facilitate the process to be as smooth as possible.

Of course, I could still have done whatever I wished without consulting the energies of the houses, and most likely nothing horrible would have happened. Asking permission is more about respect and honor than basing the entire decision on whether the houses said I was allowed to or not. I bet the look on my realtor's face would have been pretty hilarious though, if I had told her, "I'm sorry — this house won't let me move in."

The point is that when we acknowledge and include even the things considered to be inanimate in our daily lives, treating them gently with care, and keeping them and our environment neat and clean, the more the energies will have clear channels to flow back and forth, improving all levels of life. Think how it feels once you've de-cluttered your bedroom — isn't there a greater sense of ease, and a realization that you never realized how *dirty* it felt before with a mess all around?

The mainstream world can be quite bogged down with "shoulds" and "shouldn'ts," rules and regulations, but there is a deeper level to things that most are either unaware of, or do not make use of. The unseen intuitive and energetic levels very much play a part in the real world.

This is not to say that life on this planet should be *all* intuitive. That would be as unbalanced as acknowledging only the visible, tangible world.

What I call Intuitive Living is a balance — a middle ground — between the two. To live totally in the energetic or spiritual realms is too ungrounded and floaty, out of touch with the physical reality we are a part of at this time, whether we like it or not. To live totally in the solid, ordinary physical realms is *too* grounded and disconnected from the natural energies that empower all of life. Intuitive Living is a balance between the "by the book" physical world and the free-flowing and open energetic world, and is very necessary to function fully in this place.

Returning to the example of getting a new house used above, my family and I were not even looking for houses at the time. We had expected to continue renting where we were for several more years as we saved up money for a new house. Then one day, the house directly across the street from us went up for sale. Out of curiosity, I was looking up information on that house, joking to my wife, "Hey, we could just move across the street—that'd be an easy move!"

As I was on the website that listed homes for sale in our city, a beautiful home that just happened to be the size and price we would have looked for in the future unexplainably found its way onto my screen. I immediately felt and recognized the zing of energy that I feel when something is asking to be paid attention to. I could have easily ignored it, citing, "It's no use even looking—we don't have the savings for a house we'd like, we aren't even shopping for houses right now, our storage and affairs aren't cleaned out and prepared for a move," or any number of excuses.

Instead, we acknowledged the energy nudges, loaded the kids in the van, and drove out to look at the house from the curb. We all fell absolutely in love with it, and the energy connection between it and us was definitely strong—so strong, in fact, that I said, "It won't hurt anything to *try* to get this house," and called my realtor friend the very next day.

When following intuitive "nudges," it is important to trust both the energy *and* your own reading of it. Second-guessing and doubting will cause the entire thing to grow unstable, and you may even miss further clues or signs as you go along. When I sat down with my realtor, she wanted to make a list of qualities we want in a house, so she could run a search of similar houses, if this one didn't pan out. I shook my head and said, "No, we want *this* one. *This* one is our house."

From there, everything began to quickly fall into place, one thing after another: our offer was the one accepted by the seller over several others in the running, the mortgage lender we were connected with was able to very smoothly and knowledgably approve and arrange the loan paperwork even without as large a down payment as we would have normally placed, and the inspection, closing paperwork, packing, and moving process all happened on schedule, without complications, and with complete funding.

Without any prior idea or preparation that we were about to move, we effortlessly went from discovering the new house even existed, to moving *into* the new house in the span of only thirty-seven days.

On paper, if we had gone "by the book," we

should not have been able to accomplish or afford getting a new house or moving, but by listening to, trusting, and following our intuition – which is listening to the energies – just look what happened!

Once you learn to "listen" to the energies, you don't *have* to always know what you're doing. For example, when taking care of plants, you don't have to have a degree in horticulture. You can simply communicate with your plants and flowers directly, and let *them* tell you what they need – more water, less water, no water at all right now?

When waiting for an elevator (or lift, to my overseas friends) to arrive, try communicating with the machine, and see if you can feel which of the two or three cars will arrive for you, then be standing in front of the correct one already when it opens. This is especially fun to do when other people are standing waiting with you – without any visible cues, you suddenly walk over to the elevator that opens before it ever does!

Play, silliness, and humor are powerful keys to maintaining clean and clear energy flow. It's important to be able to laugh at ourselves, and not ever take things too seriously.

Make a game of trying to sense how many people are around the corner or in another room as you walk down the hall, then see if you're right when you get there. Creating little personal games for yourself will not only entertain yourself, but will exercise your intuition and keep your Flow loosened up and open.

Learning to feel energy intuitively can help you keep yourself and your loved ones safe as well. For example, I've entered many shops or events, only to turn right back around and leave again because the energy or "vibe" of the place set off warning bells in my system. This could have been a physical danger, or an energetic one, as some people unfortunately do try to misuse their empowerment to control or harm others.

I want to mention again here that we should not live in constant fear that someone is going to harm us or do anything energetically to us. Although there are those who do such things, and we should be alert to any bells or warnings we feel regarding such things, we should not go around intentionally watching for those things or expecting them. In this universe of energy we live in, we always get what we look for—we attract what we put out. Therefore, if we are paranoid or always on the lookout for someone to try to pull something, then that is exactly what we are going to find and call to ourselves. Instead, it is much easier to simply know ourselves and the feeling of our own energy system so well that anything foreign or out-of-whack will immediately trigger alarms—and even then, we can merely handle it, shove it away, or visualize a blockade wall against it, and go on our way.

I've seen many "newbies" who are just beginning to learn energy get themselves freaked out and worked up, giving in to fears and a wild imagination, but our empowerment is our empowerment—only *we* get to say what goes in our world.

Energy can only attract to energy that resonates in the same way. Repelling energies cannot coexist in the same space for long at all. If someone is throwing nasty energy at you, the only way it is going to stick and affect you is if there is some variation of that same nasty energy existing within yourself. This is not saying that you must be nasty yourself if you find yourself affected by an "attack," but saying that it is an opportunity for you to examine yourself and a chance to get to know yourself even better as a result. Look inside yourself honestly, and ask yourself exactly what inside you is helping this energy to stick. It doesn't have to be the exact same thing, but an energy within the same range of it could allow it to stick—and even fear of something like that happening is of the same energy as the thing itself.

It is vitally, vitally important to allow no fear in your system at all. Knowing yourself is the foremost key to growing strong in yourself, which eliminates all fears and unsureness within yourself.

Another way to get to know yourself better is through the use of tools, such as tarot cards, oracle cards, or the pendulum, to name a few.

Back in 2002, one of the first tools I began learning and making use of as I examined myself and searched within to analyze where I'd come from, where I was, and then choose where I wanted to go from there, was the tarot.

Many people misunderstand the purpose of the tarot cards, largely due to Hollywood and television. They believe the cards are to divine the future. While a tarot reading may suggest a possible future outcome, the true purpose and intention of the tarot is to offer insight into yourself—a tool to give you a sort of external perspective. It is always easier to see where others are possibly making harmful decisions, but far more difficult to see the same in yourself. You are simply too close to yourself to be able to see it. This is where tools may be helpful.

The definition of *divine* as a verb is "to discover." The way reading cards or any other divination tool works is by making use of intention and energy. They are instruments of discovering or revealing energy.

For example, if you are doing a reading to look into a certain question, your question is already floating around you in the form of energetic intention. As you shuffle the cards, thinking of your question, the energy of your intention interacts with the energy of the cards, working together to project the answer in the cards that are pulled from the deck and spread out. The cards are then read as a story, each card like a frame in a comic strip, to determine your answer.

Even if you have no specific question, a blanket intention such as, "What message do I most need at this time?" will offer you points to reflect and meditate on as you examine the "snapshot" of where you are, and then consciously choose how you wish to act from there.

As a present-moment self-discovery tool, the cards often mirror aspects of certain things you are working on in yourself, or *need to* work on. Intuitive readings require complete openness and honesty with yourself. You must be willing to truly look at yourself, banish all denial, and not lie to yourself.

Sometimes the things you feel, pick up on, or get in a reading will not make any sense, or you will not be able to understand it at the time, and that's perfectly all right. Sometimes the message alone is the point, and not all the "whys" of it. Trying to figure out all the whys of things that cannot be answered at the present moment can waste precious time. You simply trust the energy, reflect within, and keep moving.

Any possible futures projected in divination

readings are from looking at the snapshot of energy as it is in the present moment, and showing *potential* outcomes of those energy courses, *if unaltered or unchanged*. But energy is always in a state of shifting and flowing, and even the fact of looking at something or knowing about something can shift its flow and change its outcome. Therefore, the so-called future cannot ever be accurately predicted. Only warnings or cautions such as, "If *this* continues, then *this* may happen, and if you do not desire this, then changes are suggested."

Trying to divine a definite future is always a waste of time.

Eventually, as you become more familiar with feeling both your own energy and the energies all around yourself, you will grow to where you no longer need any tools to intuitively feel into situations. You can reach an energy stream ahead to feel how something may turn out with only your mind—but no matter how good at it you become, life must still be lived here and now, in the present moment.

To base and pattern a life solely around shifting energies that may or may not come into being is only inviting disappointment and doubt. If you take major action on something based on an intuitive reading, and then if that thread of energy does not come to fruition after all for any number of unknowable reasons, how let down and discouraged would you then feel?

As with anything, a middle balance must be maintained in order to be fully functional here. The key is to work with feeling into the energies, yet to remain unattached to the actual outcome, empowered with your life and decisions firmly in your own control. Remember: just wait and see. Keep an eye on the energies, work with them when possible, but *live* in the present, physical world.

Another danger to watch for is becoming dependent or reliant on intuitive tools. Many many times, I've seen people who begin learning to use divination tools become almost addicted to them, and afraid to make decisions of any sort without consulting their tools first.

This is the opposite of self-empowerment.

• 6 •
MYSTIC AND RELIGIOUS ENERGIES

MYSTIC, SACRED, AND RELIGIOUS systems all acknowledge the unseen supernatural or "higher" energies in our Universe.

Since the dawn of humans on this planet, I'm sure there has not been a single person who has not had at least one moment of silent marvel at the sheer vastness of this place, and of the universe at large. Questions naturally arise within us, wondering exactly what is out there.

When people began to discover they could actually *feel* the vastness and seemed to be able to communicate with this vastness, religions began to develop as explanations to these holy and sacred connections.

The unseen sensations felt greater than the people themselves, and seemed to have a personality of Its own, so concepts of gods and deities began to develop as imagery to embody the energy they were in touch with.

The energy also felt familiar or similar to how people were themselves, so it was decided that this Great Energy was what had created them, and therefore they owed the energy their lives. If everything is energy, comes from the energy, and returns to the energy, then in a sense, they were exactly right: they owed their life to what they are made of—otherwise they would have no life at this level of existence!

Everyone has always had direct access to this Great Energy, though several organizations have set up a chain-of-command system over the years where only a select few are allowed direct access to the energy, and everyone else must go through those few to get in touch with the energy. While mediators such as priests and shamans are absolutely required at certain times when extra help, assistance, or teaching is needed, it is ridiculous to say that not everyone is able to access and communicate with the very stuff they're made of. That's no different than trying to tell a fish it's not allowed to get wet while in the ocean!

To be fair, nearly every form of religion does have its mystical branch, even if its main body is not necessarily mystical. Mystics are those who have found and obtained the most direct connection to the Great Energy—and are often so alive and ecstatic from it that they are labeled crazy eccentrics. Yet when reading the words of some of the greatest mystics, such as Rumi, Hafiz, and Kabir, you can feel they really did have a beyond-the-norm understanding of life, especially in relation to the Great Energy of the Universe.

Gods, Demigods, Deities, and characters of all sorts have emerged over the eons, to give our human minds faces to personify the energies felt, to focus on or aspire to. For example, when a sense of great Love and Compassion was felt, the image of the god/goddess Kuan Yin was developed, giving a soft and gentle physical personality to that energy. In the same way, when help in defending the helpless was needed, the image of a wrathful deity, such as Mahakala, was formed to call up the energies of justice or vengeance.

Doesn't that sound like energyworking?

The purpose of many—if not all—the gods is to help our minds in visualizing whatever it is we require or wish, whether it is assistance or encouragement we need. Even the more historical figures such as Jesus Christ or Buddha Shakyamuni are embodiments of energies and concept examples to follow. Whether they did or did not literally exist as "real" people at one time does not matter. What matters is their message— and the majority of their message is in the energy they hold and convey.

I realize this is still very sticky territory at this time, as millions of people firmly believe that God or the Universe is literally an entity controlling and judging all things in existence, and that's perfectly all right—they are just as correct! Whether the Source is called God or the Great Energy, the base remains the same. In the end, it's only a matter of choosing which story you resonate with best. If someone is more comfortable with the image of a Being in the Sky creating all things, then let them visualize that how they wish. If someone else is more comfortable thinking in terms of emerging from a vast ocean of energy of which all things consist of, then let them.

Imagery and stories may differ, but the underlying energy is the heart of the matter. Fighting, arguing, and nit-picking details that are formless and unknowable from this level of existence is a complete waste of time and energy. What is called a *door* in America is called *la puerta* in Mexico, but it is still the same object that allows or blocks passage to another area. Would anyone spend lifetimes arguing this—or even kill another over it?

As mentioned before, replacing words when contemplating a concept like this is the greatest way to gain a different perspective on it, to see if it still makes sense in a another context. If it is ridiculous in another context, it is most likely ridiculous in the context in question.

The energy is the Source, creating the Creation, and the energy *is* the Creation. The two cannot be separate.

There are thousands of different gods and deities all around the world, and some religions even have many faces or personifications for the same god. This makes perfect sense. After all, I am only one man, yet at the same time I am also a son and a brother and a husband and a father and a friend and an author and an artist and an employee and a citizen and a human and a spirit simultaneously. Why wouldn't it make sense to have a face for every aspect of a deity in the same way? Different situations call for different energies, and when the only thing humans can do is apply human characteristics and explanations to things that can be felt but not seen, the natural thing to do would be to envision a personality to call in the best energy needed for the moment and purpose.

Once a certain energy is given an image or a name, it becomes very real, just as if you reach ahead of yourself on the way to the grocery store to request that an up-close parking space be created for you, and you get that parking space. The instant you think up anything, it is real on some level, whether it manifests on an energetic level, or has enough energy power behind it to manifest all the way down to the physical levels of reality. The more people acknowledge and feed an energy, the more impact it holds — look at the energy of Jesus Christ. How many people have acknowledged that energy over the last two thousand years? It's no wonder He has such power to heal and change lives!

In fact, this is what all prayer is, no matter the religion — energyworking.

The formula for prayer or manifestation is: envision, broadcast, manifest. Everything from crossing your fingers to wishing on stars to lighting candles to praying directly to God counts as prayer. In fact, the entire Law of Attraction method is nothing but prayer repackaged, if done in the correct frame of mind.

This formula applies to both negative thoughts and good-willed, beneficial thoughts, whether directed toward ourselves or others. When our every thought is springing into reality on certain levels, it is vitally important to guard our minds and our thoughts. Our every thought is a prayer, and the more perseverance and energy is poured into a prayer, the more it is pulled closer and closer into manifesting in physical reality, if circumstances allow.

Scripted prayers and mantras that are recited hold energy and power through centuries of energy being poured into them by people, just as divine personalities do. Spontaneous, free-flowing prayers from the Heart may have great power and effect on a situation, but time-tested scripts are also like magic spells with the energy they carry — if the heart and emotion is present when reciting them. As always, intention and feeling are major keys for anything. Mindless "going through the motions" will not usually get you very far at all.

There have actually been statistical studies and tests done on the power of prayer and meditation. Groups of people gathered to pray and meditate in major areas of violence, and the levels of violence surrounding them monitored. The results revealed that if the number of people praying was as little as 1% of the population the prayer would influence, clear and definite effects were able to be seen. That is relatively a very small number!

Even when you are not intentionally praying, the energy that radiates from you and your thoughts, attitudes, and intentions throughout your day affects all people and things around you — and what are you 1% of? In a family of four people, you are 25% of your family. If it takes only 1% to influence an environment, how much are you affecting your loved ones at 25%?

Your choices of attitude minute by minute are extremely important when seen in this light, don't you think?

Another act that nearly all religions make use

of is worship. Worship is just as important as prayer — it is the expression of gratefulness.

The energy of gratefulness is right beside laughter on the list of things that clear channels and energy flow very quickly. When you are expressing your thankfulness and gratitude, acknowledging and appreciating all the blessings you have, you open *la puerta* wide to allow even more blessings to flow in. Focusing on what you *do* have causes a natural gratefulness to rise. Focusing on what you do *not* have — and wishing you did have it — will shut down your channels just as quickly, causing a never-ending loop of suffering for yourself.

Rituals and symbolism are also excellent ways to acknowledge and invite the energies to flow freely in our lives. A ritual has no power in and of itself, and often has no realistic purpose, but is an outward, physical expression of an inner intention.

As long as we are on this physical level, as long as we are human, our bodies and minds are helped greatly by visuals and actions, just as we create personalities to embody the divine energies in order to better relate to and interact with them. It's not a failing if you work better with spirit guides and ceremonies, just as it's not a failing if you find you are able to accomplish what you wish without the use of these tools, or even feel hampered trying to use them.

Symbolic ritual is everywhere in our daily lives, and can be anything from changing out holiday decorations each season to throwing baby showers and funerals. Ritual helps our energy to recognize — even subconsciously — and allow the passage of time. If things like these are never paid any attention to or given honor, our energy flow may begin to become gummed up and clogged, which can in turn begin to affect other areas of our lives from our physical health to our successes and accomplishments.

Often, our hectic daily lives feel extremely overwhelming, and we can feel as if we do not have time to even slow down, much less acknowledge the flow of energy in our lives. It can feel as if we need to get away from everything in order to calm down and balance out, and it can be very tempting to want to run away to a meditation retreat in the mountains or a holy land somewhere on foreign soil.

But what many who have actually put those urges into action have found is that all their worries and stresses they were trying to get away from were right there where they ran to just the same. They did not succeed in escaping them — because the perception of these daily life things as problems or hindrances was in their own mind, and therefore went wherever they went.

The key is within your own mind.

You don't have to go anywhere to find and

touch the Great Energy in your life. It is filling the room you are sitting in right now just as much as it is filling the holiest land you could travel to.

If you believe you have no time to pay attention to and honor the energy flow of life, you will never *have* the time. In the same way, if you can realize that the energy can be acknowledged and honored in even the most mundane everyday chores, then you may find yourself living with a sense of boundless freedom and time!

When we acknowledge and make effort to respect the energies in our everyday life, our lives can become as holy as any monk or priest. We find we can feed the cats, we can scrub the toilet, we can work our corporate jobs in all its fluorescent lighting, and still live fully connected to and in communication with the Great Energy all around us.

• 7 •
YOUR ENERGY BODY

IN ADDITION TO YOUR body being made of nothing but energy, your body also consists of layers of energy, and a complete energy processing system.

Your energy body is made of essentially three major layers. The outermost layer is referred to as the *aura*, and is the electromagnetic field emitted by the pure life force voltage of your existence — your own unique energy signature created by the clustering of energy that is *you*.

Depending on your mental, emotional, and physical health in any given moment, your aura can extend from your physical body a distance of anywhere between one to eight feet (approximately 30 to 244 centimeters). If you were an astronaut in outer space, your aura would be like your spacesuit, your personal bubble of air to survive in the vacuum of space. If your spacesuit was not fully functional or even had a hole in it, you would feel the effects of that in your physical body even before your instrument panel alerted you there was a problem. Your aura can be your first alert radar as you move through your world — both sensing and reporting energetic information to you, as well as shielding you from other energies around you.

Shielding here is not meant in the same way a solid castle wall shields, for example, but more like a filter, sorting through energies around you, allowing only energy that resonates with your own system to enter. But if your energy and aura are unbalanced or unhealthy, it can be as if there are holes poked in your spacesuit.

The center layer of your energy body is your actual physical body. The physical layer is the solid manifestation of your energetic essence that is able to interact directly with other solid objects and people on this plane. This layer includes the muscles, organs, bones, and cellular structure, and is naturally the most familiar to people.

The innermost layer of your energy body is the core energy cluster that is your essence. Emotions and feelings that filter upward and affect the rest of your system are located here, and it is here that the root causes of any imbalances or issues are rooted.

The energy layer of your energy body generates and manifests all other aspects of your being. If the flow of energy at this level is blocked or bogged down, the physical cells it sustains eventually begin to crumble, and the body can begin to show signs of illness.

Aligned down the center of your physical body are energy centers that penetrate all three layers of your energy body, and regulate your flow of energy, processing both the energies you absorb from outside yourself, as well as the emotional energies you generate yourself.

These energy centers are called *chakras*. "Chakra" is an ancient Sanskrit word meaning "wheel," named for the spinning motion they appear to make as energy flows through them. The chakras are like small galaxies spinning inside the universe of your energy body, and each galaxy has its own personality, or function.

You actually have hundreds of chakras throughout your body, but there are seven major, or primary chakras, each with specific properties and colors associated. These energy centers follow your spinal column along an energetic line called the *Hara Line*. This energetic line is like a rope through your center, continuing down from you deep into Earth, and reaching infinitely up from you to the center of the Universe.

Your first chakra is associated with red, and is known as the *Root Chakra*, or Base Chakra. It rests at the bottom of your tailbone, and is the center from which your primal survival instincts rise. This is your foundation and connection to the earth. The state of this chakra determines how "grounded" or "floaty" you feel. An out of balance Root Chakra can leave you feeling insecure and disconnected. Your human encoding inherited from your parents and ancestors is found in this chakra — the "autopilot" things your body naturally knows how to do.

Your second chakra is orange, and called the *Sacral Chakra*. It is found in the center of your pelvis, and is the center for your desires, creativity, and sexuality. The survival instincts filtering up from your Root Chakra urge you to create and procreate through this chakra, and it is here you determine exactly what your preferences are — what it is you do like and do not like. You relate to others through this center, both sexually and platonically. You also "brainstorm" in the Sacral Chakra, formulating writing, painting, or any sort of creative problem-solving here. It can be thought of as the imagination center.

Third in line is your *Solar Plexus Chakra*. This chakra is yellow, and is slightly above your naval. This is your storehouse of life-force energy called *chi*. It is your command center for putting decisions into action, as well as the seat of your ego. When this chakra is out of balance, you may find yourself depressed, unable to make decisions, angry, or selfish. Depending on which way the imbalance has gone, you may find your ego under-inflated (low self-esteem) or over-inflated (egomaniac, full of yourself). In contrast to what we will see in the next chakra, an imbalanced Solar Plexus Chakra will quickly divide into separatist views of "us" and "them."

Chakra number four is in the center of your chest, and naturally called the *Heart Chakra*. This chakra is green, and quite possibly the most well known chakra, as it is globally accepted that the emotions are held in the Heart. A large part of its function is to process those emotions, filtering them as needed for your individual requirements and growth, before releasing them back into the ethers. This chakra is where your true compassion and pure Love arises, and where your natural respect for life resides. The Heart inherently knows that all of life is made of the same energy, and sees that there is no separation.

Your fifth chakra is your *Throat Chakra*, which is light blue in color. As the name suggests, this energy center is at your throat. It is your processor for honesty, authenticity, expression, and communication — which includes both listening and speaking up or speaking out. If your Throat Chakra is out of balance, you may feel unheard, unseen, powerless, fake, or frustrated.

Your *Third Eye Chakra*, or Brow Chakra is the sixth energy center, and is the color of indigo, a deeper purple-blue color. This chakra is in the center of your eyebrows, or a bit above this spot. From this chakra you receive your intuitive insights, knowledge, and visions. When this energy center is open and flowing, your clarity and understanding are sharp and true. When your Third Eye is "shut" or "blocked," you may feel confused, disoriented, or foggy.

The seventh and final primary energy center in your energy body is your *Crown Chakra*. This chakra sits at the top of your head, where your "soft spot" was as a newborn baby. Its color is bright violet or white, and serves as your connection to the Universe. When your Crown Chakra is aligned and connected, you may experience a pure, calm bliss and connectedness to everything around you. You feel your place in Life, and see that all things work together for the best possible outcome. From this center, you are able to "download" information from higher vibration energy sources, and translate and communicate them to others in the vibration of this earthly plane.

When any of your chakras are not functioning correctly, or if your energy flow is low or completely blocked, your system cannot operate at maximum capacity. Just as your physical body does not function if you neglect to feed it healthy foods or do not allow it enough sleep and rest, your energy body also begins to exhaust if you do not give it the attention and care it requires.

A chakra can also become *over* active or overloaded. And again, the same example applies — overstuffing your physical body with food can harm it just as much as under feeding it.

Some causes of energy blockages and chakra imbalances are negativity, fear, stress, crisis, and fatigue. Holding on to, or "stuffing down," emotions rather than processing and releasing them is another common way the balance can be overthrown, as well as unhealthy attachments to other people, such as ex-lovers or family.

Everyone is empathic to a degree, but if those who are more empathically sensitive are not adequately shielded and grounded energetically, they can easily be thrown off balance by absorbing the energies of other people and places, taking the energies on as their own.

If imbalances in energy flow continue long enough, they can begin to manifest as illness in your physical body. Emotional bottling-up is one of the leading causes of illness and dis-ease, whether it is anger, sadness, fear, or even happiness, if you are not allowed to express it.

The language of the energy body is feelings and visions. You must sense and feel what is being shown and communicated to you by your energy body, and you communicate *back* to these levels of yourself in the same way. This is why it is extremely important to consciously be aware of and choose your thoughts—especially thoughts about your own self. Your energy body listens to and obeys whatever it is you are telling it to do. This is how people who want to feel sick in order to get out of something they don't want to do can literally make themselves sick, and why those with high self-esteem seem so confident and strong.

If our thoughts are creating our very being, then why would anyone willingly destroy themselves with negative thoughts directed at themselves?

• 8 •
LEARNING TO FEEL ENERGY

ALL THINGS BEGIN WITH yourself, and it is no different with learning to feel energy. If you have no base line reference point on yourself, you will never be able to sense any distinctions of anything outside yourself. If you do not know yourself openly and honestly from the inside out, you will have difficulty determining anything else.

Methods of getting to know yourself can include anything from meditation to journaling — anything that points you to you and how you feel under "normal" conditions.

Your body and mind's interpretations of energy are going to be different from anyone else's, which is a fantastic thing, as no one has any right to say you or anyone else is doing it the "wrong" way.

Many who feel energy in their physical bodies describe the sensations of energy as a tingling or a heat or a chill. You may find your personal experience to be something completely different, and it is entirely up to you to determine or "decode" what your "signals" are. Signals can be any sort of thing or sensation anywhere in your body or mind. No one but you will be able to realize and understand your personal signals — and the only way for you to learn your own signals is by experiencing them and staying alert to what is going on around you at the time you recognize you are receiving a signal.

Begin to pay close attention to your body everywhere you go. How do certain places make you feel inside? Do some places feel heavier, and some lighter? Does anywhere feel creepy or sickening? Where does it feel comfortable and inviting to you? How do certain people or their actions make you feel?

Remember as many details and their associated sensations as you can, and next time you feel the same sensation, look at what is happening around you — it may very well be the same sort of thing that triggered the signal before, and then you will have decoded one of your energy body's signals to communicate with you.

The difference in places and environments is felt because you and your energy are one frequency of vibration, and other places and people are each vibrating at different frequencies. Some of these vibrations are closer to your own frequency, and more compatible, while others are farther from your own.

This is like your own personal, built-in guidance system. There is no "right" thing to feel, and even the same sensation can mean different things to different people. A heat sensation could indicate something is "wrong" or unbalanced to one person, while a sensation of heat could indicate something "right" or spot-on to someone else.

Once you have a thorough, conscious knowledge of yourself and exactly how things personally feel to you, you will be able to differentiate energy you pick up on that is not from yourself.

Eventually, even when you are going about your business, not even thinking about energies, you may suddenly become aware of a tingle at the base of your skull, or a twitch in a certain muscle, directing you to pause and take a quick look at where you are or what is going on around you at that moment. Perhaps there will be a message for you, or maybe something you need to do for yourself or another in need.

But you are also not helplessly at the mercy of your guidance system and signals, either — you always have the final say on how you experience energies. If you do not like the signal your body gives you for a certain thing, simply ask your body that it be changed. You can even specify exactly what you'd like to feel for each situation, if you like.

For example, when playing a guitar, there can be more than one way to fret the strings with your fingers to create a certain chord to strum. If you decide that it's too difficult or feels uncomfortable for your fingers to contort into one way for a particular chord, you can retrain yourself to fret it using your fingers in a different order on the strings, whatever feels best for you personally — there is no wrong way.

If a signal is coming across to your awareness as pain, you do not have to keep it that way. Gently ask your energy body and signal system (all energy has its own consciousness remember!) that it change that signal to something that does not feel like it hurts you.

Intentionally generating energy is also something everyone is able to do and feel. This sort of energy is even more tangible to our physical bodies, and can feel quite physical itself.

One way I began learning to sense tangible energy was by simply holding one hand over the other hand, palms facing. I activated my visualizations, and intended that energy would gather into a ball between my hands, until I could actually feel an energy ball there.

Once I was familiar with that sensation and able to create it easily at will, without thinking about it much, I began experimenting with stretching it—seeing how far I could "grow" the energy between my hands, and still feel it. I discovered I could still feel the energy as far as I could reach, and could even feel it between my hand and the hand of a friend as we separated across the distance of an entire room!

I experimented in any way I could think of. I juggled the energy ball from one hand to the other, tossed it across the room, and touched it to my different chakras, seeing how everything felt, and got a feel for working with energy.

The more you become aware of just how energetic everything everywhere around you is, the more your perceptions and viewpoints begin to shift—and the more connected to everything you feel. You begin to realize you are never alone, and that you are always just one piece of a gigantic whole that you can access at any time you need a boost or touch.

You can also use the same practice of moving energy with your intentions and visualizations to experience the energy of the Universe personally connecting with you.

Close your eyes and imagine the expanse of the Universe above you. Visualize a shaft of Its pure, primal energy coming down and entering your body through your Crown Chakra. You can do or say anything you like to "activate" the flow and communicate with your mind that you are now in a space of experiencing an energy greater than your single energy body.

Gently open yourself to the experience until you feel the energy at the top of your head. Once you become aware of it, allow yourself to sit with it fully. How does it feel to you? What sensations can you describe? What is your personal signal that the energy is flowing? A tingling? A heat? A subtle pressure on your head? Become familiar with this feeling, so you will always know when your personal connective "stream" is activated.

When you are comfortable and familiar with the sensation of drawing energy into your Crown Chakra, shift your focus to your shoulders and arms. Feel the energy running into your head, down your arms, and to your hands. Allow it to continue flowing down your legs and into your feet, until your entire body is connected with the energy of the entire Universe.

The more you grow used to physically feeling this energy, and are able to start and stop it at will, the easier it will be for you to gather energy between your hands and experiment with moving energy around.

I want to note here that the energy is always present. You are not so much "starting" and "stopping" the energy as you are turning your awareness to the energy and away from the energy. It is actually an acknowledging and recognizing of what has always been there all along. The ancient Celtic people had an encircling practice called *caim* representing this, in which they would draw a circle around themselves to symbolize the presence of God. They did not invoke this prayer as a call for God to come from a separate place to where they were to protect them, but to acknowledge and ritually bring to their own awareness the fact of what was already an ever-present reality.

Again, moving energy is powered by intention and visualization. Your thoughts are pure energy, just as everything else, creating waves and vibrations that affect the environment around you, however subtle or obvious their manifested result is. When you imagine something, it becomes real.

Create an energy ball between your hands, open your hands, and hold them palm up, side by side. Focus your attention on the ball, willing it to shift from one palm to the other. Then shift it back. Feel the movement of the energy. How does the flow feel to you? Pay close attention to the sensations you feel, and become familiar with your personal indications of energy movement.

Let loose, have fun, and play around with it. Try anything you think of. Spread your hands farther apart. Juggle the ball higher, behind your back, through the solid wood of a table—

anything!

To play is to explore and learn.

Try placing your palms together, in "prayer pose," and see what you feel. Can you feel the energy cycling around and around your arms through the connection of your palms? This is a quick and powerful way to balance your own energy whenever you're in need.

Energy is sensed not only via the senses of the physical body, but intuitively via the mind and energy body. I often explain this as "feeling without feeling," or "seeing without seeing." This sort of feeling energy makes use of your Third Eye Chakra.

When you use your Third Eye to look at things energetically, you can "see" your chakras or other energetic essences and bodies of things and people around you in your own symbolic interpretations. This is no different than the way you see things with your physical eyes. Your physical eyes register the light bouncing off a "solid" object, and feeds that information to your brain. Your brain then looks at the information, and compares it to all its previously archived shapes and images. When it finds a match, or near-match, it recalls the label for that match—its "name."

The world of energy works the same way, but you are bypassing the steps of the physical eyes sending their sensory perceptions to the nervous system, and then to the brain. Instead, you are using your mind's eye to perceive and send the information about something directly to the brain. This is much like when you recall a memory of something that happened, or visualize the view from your favorite park bench or meditation space—you can see that view clearly in your mind, though it is not physically in front of you in this moment.

Just as your physical reactions are influenced by the life experiences you've had, and the responses you've developed from those experiences, (such as "I don't really like to be tickled today because this person who always tickled me when I was a child really bothered me") your mental visions and symbolisms are also determined by these experiences. This is also how your dreams work as you sleep—your mind interprets and translates the energies you are processing as you rest into symbols and images it can understand.

Perhaps instead of a ball in your hands, the energy you gather feels more like a box. Maybe instead of tossing the energy ball across the room, your mental visualization works better for you to imagine it as if it is a laser beam you are blasting out, or a spider web type of energy shooting from your hand like Spiderman.

The same way you paid attention to and got to know your body signals is the same way you

get to know your personal energetic symbolism —
your own secret code between the Universe and
yourself.

• 9 •
HEALING WITH ENERGY

ENERGY PLAYS A HUGE factor in our health and well-being. If our energy is agitated or out of balance, and allowed to continue that way, it will begin to manifest in our physical body, affecting our ability to function fully, and will only spiral downward from there.

Just as the attitudes and energy you choose to emit each hour of your day can affect and determine the tone of the environment around you, the attitude and energy you embody or allow to thrive in your system also affects your personal energy field in even greater ways.

If you hold on to resentment or anger, that energy acts like an acid that will slowly eat you away from the inside out, and compound more and more negativity in you and around you.

If you choose to look to and hold more

positive energies of hope and love, no matter what else is going on around you, those energies will attract more and more of the same, and a natural health and graceful flow will surround your life.

Energy can affect our physical bodies in ways that baffle doctors. There are countless stories of miraculous recoveries like cancers suddenly going away on their own, and people never expected to wake from comas or walk again doing so against all odds and expectations.

For example, as I also shared in my book *Lightworker: A Call to Authenticity*, I was the personal assistant of a quadriplegic man for a time, shuttling him to doctor appointments, running errands, answering emails and phone calls, and helping him with his physical therapy exercises. This man had fairly recently become paralyzed, and had previously been a well-known dancer and dance teacher. His paralyzation had set in extremely quickly and quite mysteriously. He had been to see specialist doctors all over the country, and not a one of them could determine what was wrong with him. There had been no accident or event of any kind that would have caused such an effect on his nervous system, so they were utterly perplexed as his condition continued to deteriorate.

As I got to know him and talk with him, I learned that his ex-wife had left him for one of his own dance students, and although they still had a friendly relationship from sharing a daughter together, he held a deep bitterness and resentment inside regarding the choices of his wife. That had been *his* wife, and he still loved her more than anything, even though she had essentially betrayed him.

It was shortly after this event in his life that his condition had begun to set in. I realized that the energy and emotion he harbored and clung to had begun to shift his energy from the inside, eating away at him until it began to display visible signs in his physical body as a complete paralyzation even without the presence of a disease or brain injury. His body simply began to shut down.

Unfortunately, he was never able to release that resentment and anger, and come to terms with what had happened. He eventually lost the battle, and his life. That is the power and importance of energy in our lives.

If you are feeling sick or out of balance, energy can be moved and used with the same visualization and intention methods mentioned in previous chapters.

Within your own body, your breath is your most powerful energy mover — think about how naturally you heave a big sigh when you are trying to refresh or rejuvenate yourself.

One very effective way I've found to help my

body fight off any sickness the moment I become aware of it is to breathe it out. To breathe out energy that is making you feel sick — whether it is a physical virus you are coming down with, or you are experiencing an energetic influence — visualize the energy of whatever does not belong inside you gathering up into a single ball as you inhale deeply, then visualize and feel that energy exiting your body as you exhale just as deeply.

I think it is most likely more the intention and willpower of this exercise that removes the unwanted energy than the literal breathing it out, but such ritual actions definitely add power to our wishes.

You can freely repeat this as often as you feel is needed, but keep in mind it is not an alternative to a doctor's advice or service — always be wise and consult your doctor's care when needed.

Your chakras are the primary energy processing centers for your body, and you will naturally feel your best and be able to handle situations presented to you by life easier when they are clear and functioning fully — your energetic hygiene is just as important as taking care of your physical body!

The exercises and examples for learning to feel energy given in the previous chapter come into use when you need to move or work on your energy body — to heal yourself.

"Activate" your energy flow from the Universe at large. Feel it run through and fill your entire body.

Once you are aware of the energy running strongly, pull the energy into your hands like when you collected a ball in your palms. Feel that the energy is coming in through your Crown Chakra, down your arms, and into your hands — it is not your own energy you use, but the energy of the Universe flowing *through* you and filling you.

Now, place your hands on each chakra in turn and begin giving — moving — energy to yourself, at each of your chakras by visualizing the energy moving and flowing from your hands. See what you feel as you work with each of your energy centers. Pay close attention to what emotions arise in response at each chakra — but don't just feel them, *look* at them. Sit with them. Open yourself completely to them without any fear. Any feelings and emotions that may come up are being presented to you in order to be seen, processed, and, if necessary, released. Remember, you are not only doing this to practice feeling and working with energy — you are doing this to heal yourself. You are doing energy healing.

Begin with your Crown Chakra, at the top of your head. Place your hands on or over the energy center, and feel the energy increasing here. As the energy passes through your hands and into your Crown, what feelings arise? How does it feel to your head? How does it feel to your hands? Does the energy feel as if it is coming out of your palm, your fingertips, both, or some other way entirely?

Next, move to your Third Eye Chakra. I have discovered over time that sometimes different people's chakras are slightly higher or lower than the exact traditional textbook position. If you are not sure of your exact energy center, use the sense of feeling energy you've been practicing to pinpoint where it is. Move your hand slowly up and down the general area, feeling for the intuitive "ding" of locating it. I personally feel this as a prick in the base of my skull, at my pineal gland, but you will feel your own indication. Once you have found it, and feel it, begin flowing the energy to this chakra as well, paying attention to how it feels, and what emotions arise.

Do the same with each of your energy centers as you move down the line to Throat Chakra, Heart Chakra, Solar Plexus Chakra, Sacral Chakra, and Root Chakra. Spend as much time with each as you feel you need to. Let the energy tell you when it's done and time to move to the next. Experiment with any sort of ideas you get, paying attention to what seems to work best for you, and what does not. Even when you find and settle on an effective method, you can change it later, if you need to. Nothing is set in stone, and, in fact, a flexibility and openness to "no single set way" is very important in energy work.

Remember to remain open to any visual images you may receive as you go along. If and when you see something at a certain energy center, take a deep breath, and search within yourself for what this symbolism could be trying to show you. Watch for blockages, but not *overly* watchful or concerned about them — we often find what we look for by creating it to find in the first place. Instead, simply remain open, and allow the energy to flow and speak for itself. This will take practice, but it can be easily done.

If you get a symbolic image of something, you can ask a series of yes or no questions to narrow things down and determine exactly what is being revealed. For example, if you feel that what you are seeing could be a representation of a block in your energy flow, you could ask, "Is this thing supposed to be here?" and then intuitively feel for the answer. If you feel a "no" in response, then you can use your visualization to do anything you imagine to take care of it. Pull out the plug that is blocking the flow, dissolve the stickiness, melt the frozen energy — whatever you think of to apply to whatever you see.

For example, if you receive an image of a snake wrapped around your chakra, that could mean any number of things. To some, a snake represents harm, yet to others snake represents life, such as on the medical caduceus symbol. But neither of these mean there is a literal snake coiled around your chakra. The energy will communicate to you in images your mind will translate according to your own personal symbolisms, so you understand what is going on in your own way.

Some people see no specific images at all, but merely see different spots or colors of energy — or even nothing at all. It's all up to you as an individual.

All things must be run through your own intuitive filter — never simply assume. Asking yourself simple yes or no questions will help you feel into each possibility that occurs to you, and paying attention to your personal signals will help you narrow things down to the most likely answer.

As another example, you may ask, "Is this chakra *open* too wide?" and may feel the response for "No." You could then ask, "Is this chakra too *closed*?" and may feel your response for "Yes." You can keep digging and poke around to try to figure out *why* the chakra became blocked.

In my book *The Natural Healer's Guide,* I call this series of yes or no questions the Pinpoint Method, and it can be used to intuitively find the best way for anything, anywhere.

The most important thing is to trust yourself.

Throw wide your imagination, and do not second-guess what it is you are seeing and doing. Your first thought is usually the correct thought. Intuition is not mental. Your mind is programmed to find the rational and logical, and often cannot easily wrap itself around the concepts of energy healing and energy work. Trying to operate from the mental level will always trip you up and instill doubts. The only job your mind has in this work is remaining open to the information coming from the emotional and energetic bodies, recognizing the data as the same sort it receives from the physical organs, and translating those signals into images you personally understand.

When you've finished giving energy to each of your chakras, stay very still, breathe deeply, and feel how your mind and body now feel as a whole. How does it compare to before you gave yourself an energy healing?

You can do this—or any portion of this—as often as you like, anytime and anywhere you need to. You can never circulate too much energy.

Many people believe or are told that they need to obtain some sort of certification or degree in order to do energy healing, but I say that's ridiculous. Energy is free, energy is everything, and energyworking is natural to everyone, for every use. Why should the healing abilities of it be only for the exclusive few?

There are many different programs or "name brands" of energy healing available, and all methods are merely systems of channeling energy – they are not the energy itself. No one can own the energy of the Universe. If you feel attracted to a specific energy healing modality, then by all means pursue that course of study.

Energy healing can help shake loose and bring up the issues that most need to be dealt with inside yourself, as well as help instill the courage and empowerment to squarely face these issues.

Healing energy is holistic in nature, meaning it seeks the root cause of an issue rather than temporarily "slapping a bandage on it." It delves to the deepest corners of the problem, and begins to bring the core issue to the surface for processing.

Energy healing can help to relieve and heal physical pain, and can also be used to reduce stress, depression, and emotional suffering.

Energy healing is never a substitute for medical care of any kind. It definitely compliments and enhances other forms of treatment and therapy, and can be used while on medication, but it should never replace medication prescribed by your doctor.

In extreme cases, such as a broken bone, you do not want to run healing energy to the area until after the bones have been set back into place correctly by a doctor. Energy works very quickly, and the tissues may begin to set in the wrong place, causing difficulties later on. Always consult a doctor in these cases.

It is also important to note that healing does not always mean restoring things back to the same state they were in previously. Sometimes healing could require simply accepting that something has changed, such as the loss of a loved one, whether to death, or to an ending of a relationship. Sometimes what is needed for healing is to own up to actions, and take responsibility for something that has happened. There are infinite combinations that could create the need for healing.

These basic methods of healing with energy can also be done on the energy body of others as well as yourself. Simply go through the routine lined out above, (or your own routine you develop) but look at and feel into their chakras rather than your own.

For ethical reasons, I recommend you do not actually touch the other person during an energy healing session, unless you are a close personal relative or in an intimate relationship with them. The energy can flow through your hands and where it needs to go simply by hovering over the area being healed.

If you are approached by someone asking for

an energy healing, you can first "check in" with yourself, and intuitively feel into if this is something you should do or not. If you feel a caution or a "no" for any reason, do not hesitate to say so—and *definitely* do not feel guilty about saying no. The Universe is unlimited in its resources, and you are *never* the one-and-only last chance for anything anywhere to happen. If not you, then another option will step up to be presented to them. There is never anything to feel guilty about.

In the same way, if you can do something to help or heal a situation, you do it. But if you cannot do anything for the situation, you let it go, and move on. Never ever allow guilt to bloom inside you. It is *not* your job to help everyone, and no one would be able to, even if they tried. You help who you can, and wish the best—which is sending energy—to those you cannot help. This in no way means you do not care about them, but is simply acknowledging the reality that you are not able to help every single person you meet.

There are obvious ethics to follow if you are working with others energetically. There is a deep trust to uphold, so others have a pure and safe space that will allow them to open to you for assistance in healing. If their vulnerability is taken advantage of for your own ulterior or selfish motives, you could cause them to leave with much more damage than they brought in with them to begin with.

When working with others, you never ever judge them for any disability or ailment they may have, whether physical or energetic. Everyone can draw or create anything from their energy and experiences, and there is no way to know exactly what they've been through that created the unbalance. It could just as easily have been caused by uncontrollable circumstances as it could have been caused at their own hand. You don't know.

Long-distance energy healings are also possible. The person you are doing an energy healing on does not have to be physically in front of you. This is possible because of the way all things are made of the same energy, and are connected as a single whole. Pieces of that whole can be located from any other point.

Finding a person remotely and sending healing energy to them works a bit like making a phone call. You tell your phone the number of the person you want to call, and when you hit "Dial," the electronic and digital lines do the rest, searching the network of connections until the connection you requested is located, and your call is connected to only that connection. In a long-distance healing, you "call up" the energy of the person you will be working on, and then use your Third Eye Chakra to tune in to the line of energy traced for you. In reality, this is how energy healing works whether the client is physically in front of you, or three thousand miles away.

You cannot heal anyone. No matter how much you care about them, everyone must do their own healing work for themselves, and must be ready and willing to do whatever it takes to heal. If they are not truly ready to release whatever it is causing them unbalance, whatever effects your energy healing may have will be temporary. There are many people who are merely after the feel-good high that energy healing often induces. If the desire to do the work necessary for themselves is not present, the healing will also not be found. No one else can do their work for them.

In the same way, you cannot diagnose or cure others. You are only a channel for life force energy to flow through—a mediator for the healing energies of the Universe, to try to help empower the recipient to heal themselves.

Again, as an energy healer, you never interfere in the medical treatments of others, and you absolutely do not suggest that anyone discontinue medications or counseling.

It is very important to keep yourself as cleared and balanced as possible, so the energy of the Universe can flow through you as unhindered as possible. But all is not lost if you do happen to still be processing through something in your own life at the time you are led to hold a healing session for others—the Universe is pure, and as you step aside, the Universe will not only flow where healing is needed, but it will also assist you in your own personal situation at the same time.

When your energy healing session with another person is complete, always remember to release any energetic ties that may have been established between you. When you do energy work on others, cords or attachments to the one you are working on can form, and must be cut and released afterwards, or you may end up "carrying" them around with you, weighing you down with burdens that are not your own.

These attachments can be cut with a simple intention and visualization, such as visualizing any lingering ties being cut with giant energetic scissors, or even simply saying, "I now cut and release any cords and ties that have established between so-and-so and myself." Feel the connection release from your energy field.

Perhaps the most important question to ask yourself is why you want to do energy healing. Do you feel "led" to it, as if it is calling to you from your very bones, or is your desire more from a place of ego—that "cool factor" of being able to brag and tell people you are an energy healer? Is it to accelerate your own healing? Is it to create another avenue for the compassion of your Heart to express itself to others?

Complete honesty with yourself, and complete knowing of yourself makes a world of difference in these areas.

Authenticity is a very important part of being an energy worker. You must be able to be firmly and strongly secure in yourself and your own boundaries. You must be able to tell someone "No" when needed, whether it is to take care of and not overextend yourself, or if it is because you sense they are not truly doing their part of the work in order to heal.

If you have difficulty telling anyone no when they are wanting something, you may find yourself backed into a miserable corner, and your own self suffering and in need of healing.

• 10 •
CURIOUSER AND CURIOUSER

An OPEN MIND AND child-like imagination are your best friends in all forms of working with energy, followed by a confident trust and faith in yourself. Remember, there are no wrong ways or wrong answers for any of it—every bit of it is completely your own way, your own world.

Be curious about everything, and don't be afraid to experiment with anything you think up. Curiosity never *really* killed any cats, did it?

Everything is connected to everything, and everything participates and affects the same pool of energy. Anything you discover or create contributes to this pool, and becomes available for the further expansion of the whole—or toward the further tearing down of the whole. There are even schools of thought that feel everyone is so interconnected that no change can fully happen until it happens to everyone. In this train of thought, I cannot heal without *everyone* healing. I as an individual piece of the whole may be able to be a healed cell myself, but as a piece of the whole, if there are others still unhealed, there is a fragment of myself that remains unhealed. This is what inspires the Buddhist heroes known as Bodhisattvas—they understand the Oneness of the entire Universe, and even though they have personally attained enlightenment, they have consciously chosen to remain and assist all others in their climb, in any way needed.

And so your curiosity can be fueled not only by your own thirst, but also by your love and compassion for all the Universe. You can legitimately feel that everything you do to grow and further yourself, is for all others as well.

Many people have a nearly overwhelming feeling that they are not from this place. They feel they don't quite fit in, and that this planet is not their home. They search for and claim labels such as Starseed and Indigo, trying to define this feeling. I feel that what they are sensing is their own divinity, their bigger, true, Universal self peeking out. They are touching their connection and Oneness with the Universe.

Feelings like this make it very hard to be here at times—and it is difficult on this level of existence to be both human and divine simultaneously. I have found over the years that reshaping your lifestyle to acknowledge and work with energy as a part of your daily routine definitely puts you in a deeper and direct touch with the Universal connection, and greatly helps with the feelings of isolation and loneliness.

Some other excellent tools to help you find your balance among the shifting energies are objects like crystals, stones, and incense.

There are thousands of beautiful and very effective crystals available, from all parts of the world. Each has its own metaphysical and energetic properties, enhancing certain energy characteristics in yourself, and helping with healings and clearings. Many books and websites are easily available to research which stones will best compliment every need.

The aromas, properties, and intentions of incense are powerful energy movers as well. Different scents very clearly trigger deep-seated encoding in our DNA and energy, producing instant effects for the intended results the incense is being burned for. Burning a cluster of white sage, for example, will clear and purify the energy of a place—or even your body—quite quickly.

Objects can absorb and hold energy from people and places just as easily as your body can. The older an object is, and the more places it has been and owners it has had, the more likely this is to occur. I personally have to be sure to shield and release excess energy whenever I go into places like antique stores, thrift stores, and flea markets. Such tight gathering of so many different energies can be extremely overwhelming, and even nauseating at times.

The energy clinging to an object *can* be cleaned or "reprogrammed" though. The same way energy can be used to clear an object is the same way it can be used to "program" intentions and purposes *in* to it. An example of this could be if you don't have a crystal that helps you clear and balance, you could program your writing pen to hold the energy that clears and balances you. That way, every time you pick up your pen, you will get the same effects as if you were holding a crystal.

For that matter, you can also program the energy around you in the same way. You can create a bubble around yourself to be able to stay balanced inside of, or you can affect the actual physical properties of the air around you. If it's the cold of winter where you are, you can pull warm energy around yourself, or you can draw cool air to yourself if it's the heat of summer. You can do anything you can think of with energy.

It's even possible to use energy to hide yourself, as if you had Harry Potter's invisibility cloak, or a Star Trek cloaking device. But just because something is possible does not mean it is necessarily wise, especially when it involves layers of energy, and affects countless unknowable physical interactions.

I once experienced this lesson in a bit of a jolting way. I had been summoned to the local courthouse for jury duty, and while I sat in the holding room waiting for them to call the next round of randomly selected names for the next court case, I decided to play with and practice some energy work. Since I didn't really mind getting a day off work to sit downtown and read my book, but did not really want to serve on a jury, I set the intention to be wrapped in invisibility, thinking this would keep my name from being pulled from the hat.

Lunch came and went, and I seemed to have been successful, as my name had not been called. The afternoon slipped away, and the officials finally determined they had all the jurors they needed for the week, and dismissed all who remained, saying we did not need to return the next day.

I went to work as normal the next day, and was quite pleased with my little trick, until my cell phone rang. It was the bailiff from the courthouse, demanding to know where I was and why I hadn't reported to the courtroom that morning and had I even shown up to the selection day yesterday as mandatory by law.

I explained that I *had* been present the day before, told him exactly where in the waiting room I had been sitting, what card games other jurors had been playing, that my name had *not* been called, and that I had been released and told I did not need to return. I said I had even turned in my name badge to the lady at the front desk on my way out, and he could check that they had it in that box.

The bailiff grunted, then put the judge himself on the phone. I explained the whole thing again to the judge, and said that I could be down there in twenty minutes if needed, despite the misunderstanding.

Fortunately, the judge decided he believed me, and that there had been a mistake somewhere. He dismissed me, and said I did not need to come down.

It seemed my invisibility energy wrap *had* worked, but not in the way I had intended. Apparently, it had *not* stopped my name from being drawn, but it *had* hidden my name on the list as the bailiff called the names out. My name had been on the list, but skipped over.

Since that day, I have been extremely careful about trying to intentionally manipulate energies in ways like that. There are far too many variables and layers involved, and absolutely no way to account for and specify for them all. Hiding yourself from an unjust apartment complex office after you move could block your security deposit refund from reaching you as well. Hiding yourself from police as you break the speed limit down the highway could also hide you from other drivers, who may smash into you as they change lanes, not knowing you are in the way.

Energy is not to be used for such personal gains, any more than it is able to be bullied rather than worked with in partnership.

As you go about your daily life, you *will* sometimes feel your healing energy stream turn itself on. It is the pure energy of the Universe you flow through yourself, and the energy of the Universe knows exactly where a concentration of healing energy is most needed.

If you enter a building or environment that needs the higher vibration of Universal energy, and you are an open channel for that, the energy can naturally turn on and pour from you as you go about your business.

In fact, you do not even have to do an actual energy healing session to help others—it can be done silently and privately, wherever you are, and whatever you're doing, whether you're a hairdresser running energy as you work on someone's hair, or a grocery store clerk programming your customer's items as you ring them up. Even a simple, "May they be well," beamed in the direction of someone can hold all the healing energy required.

Your mind and ego will oftentimes want to be

in control and want to know all the reasons, details, and *whys* of a thing, but that is not always the point. It is certainly all right to be curious and want to find out all you can about what is going on or what you are observing or feeling or picking up on, but the answers to these things may not be knowable, for any number of reasons, and precious time and energy can be lost if you allow yourself to obsess too much over it. You will always be shown and told only what you need to know for the present moment in time — no more, and no less. Perhaps an answer is not revealed to you because of a personal trigger you have that could activate a fear within yourself if you were to know. If that example were the case, then it could actually harm you more than help you to know the answer at the moment.

Hindsight is 20/20, the saying goes — and that is quite true here as well. Sometimes there is no way to know why something has happened while still in the present moment, but later, down the road, the bigger picture is exposed. "Wait and see," is truly one of the most powerful mantras.

On the other end of that, the importance of staying open and willing to see things the way they truly are is very important in working with energy. If you have preconceived expectations, you increase your chances of missing a clue or misinterpreting a signal. You will also be setting yourself up for the possibility of disappointment and self-doubt, if what you are expecting is not what actually happens.

If you see colors at each of the chakras as you do an energy healing, be prepared to find that they may not always be the same colors every time. Color is only one symbolic way the energy communicates with you, and can shift around to tell you exactly what is going on and what needs to be done.

For example, let's say you're doing an energy healing on a friend, and you see the traditional blue at the Throat Chakra and the typical green at the Heart Chakra. If you're working at their Throat Chakra, and sense pieces of green in their Throat, this could be an indication that they have been working on trying to voice something from their Heart, or maybe that they have *not* been voicing their truth from the Heart.

Above all, your intentions and motives are at the heart of working with energy. Energy responds to that bottom line, even you are consciously unaware of it yourself. Complete honesty with yourself and a commitment to authenticity are vitally important in all things — especially the more aware you become of the energies all around you.

The recurring message and theme of the Spiderman comic book storylines is "With great power comes great responsibility," and this is indeed true when it comes to working with energy in our lives.

True empowerment is knowing yourself completely, the ability to stand firm in yourself and your integrity, and possessing the self-control to consciously choose your actions and thoughts, no matter what else is happening around you.

The energy you and all things are made of is present to help you be as empowered as possible, day and night, around the clock.

May you be well, and find all you need in this moment.

Everybody understands
the single drop merging into the ocean.

One in a million comprehends
the ocean merging into a single drop.

— Kabir

May you be blessed beyond measure!

ABOUT THE AUTHOR

I AM LLOYD MATTHEW THOMPSON, and I've always been naturally aware of energies my entire life—even while growing up in my strict religious family home of nine children, of which I was the oldest.

I've studied energy work in general since 2003, and energy healing specifically since 2007, attaining my Reiki Grand Master level with nationally known energy healer and shaman Phyllis Maxey.

I have been an intuitive reader since 2002, working local metaphysical and spirit fairs, offering energy healing, tarot card readings, and intuitive artwork readings, which combined my life-long artistic abilities with my intuitive "psychic" abilities.

Raised Baptist, I have since explored, experienced, and been shaped by many other paths, including Buddhism, Shamanism, Paganism, and New Age. Whether writing, painting, drawing, or teaching, reflections of all these can be found within each body of my work.

I have written for various metaphysical and holistic blogs and magazines, both locally and globally, and have created my publishing project, *Starfield Press*, (**www.StarfieldPress.com**) as a platform for both my works and the works of others, fiction and nonfiction.

I am the author of *Lightworker: A Call to Authenticity* and *The Natural Healer's Guide*, as well as *The Healer: A Novel*.

My intention in all my work is to inspire and uplift, encouraging all toward self-empowerment and the highest, most authentic states possible.

Much Love to you all.

Lloyd Matthew Thompson
Oklahoma City, OK

Books by Lloyd Matthew Thompson

THE ENERGY OF GOD

WISE ONE:
THE SONG OF MANJUSHRI

THE NATURAL HEALER'S GUIDE

LIGHTWORKER:
A CALL TO AUTHENTICITY

ENERGYWORKER:
A CALL TO EMPOWERMENT

THE HEALER: A NOVEL

ROOT: A NOVELLA

AURA: A SHORT STORY

LIGHT
WORKER

A CALL TO AUTHENTICITY

BESTSELLING AUTHOR OF *ENERGYWORKER*
LLOYD MATTHEW THOMPSON

Look for *Lightworker: A Call to Authenticity*
Only from **Starfield Press**!

"Enlightening, empowering...
5-Star information!"

THE
NATURAL
HEALER'S
GUIDE

BESTSELLING AUTHOR OF *LIGHTWORKER*
LLOYD MATTHEW THOMPSON

Look for *The Natural Healer's Guide*
Only from **Starfield Press**!

www.ingramcontent.com/pod-product-compliance
Lightning Source LLC
Chambersburg PA
CBHW060018050426
42448CB00012B/2798